The Phoenix Living Poets

THE WHITE BIRD

THE
WHITE BIRD

By

NORMAN MacCAIG

CHATTO AND WINDUS

THE HOGARTH PRESS

1973

Published by
Chatto and Windus
with The Hogarth Press Ltd
42 William IV Street
London W.C.2

★

Clarke, Irwin & Co. Ltd
Toronto

ISBN 7011 1918 7

© Norman MacCaig 1973

Printed in Great Britain by
Lewis Reprints Ltd.,
The Brown, Knight and Truscott Group
London and Tonbridge

CONTENTS

MILNE'S BAR

Cigarette smoke floated
in an Eastern way
a yard above the slopped tables.

The solid man thought
nothing could hurt him
as long as he didn't show it —

a stoicism of a kind. I
was inclined to agree with him,
having had a classical education.

To prove it, he went on telling
of terrible things that had
happened to him —

so boringly, my mind
skipped away among the glasses
and floated, in an Eastern way,

a yard above the slopped
table; when it looked down,
the solid man

was crying into his own mouth.
I caught sight of myself
in a mirror

and stared, rather admiring
the look of suffering
in my middle-aged eyes.

STAGES

The wave's grip loosened and it fell
off the rock, leaving in cracks and crevices
snuffling sponges of yellow froth.

I sat on stones that had been taken
from a derelict house to patch
a house now derelict.

Through its staved walls I could see
the wrecks of objects that had been made
from the wrecks of ships.

It made me boast of me,
not quite derelict, not quite a wreck, not yet
lodged in a cosy crevice.

I walked off, striking my foot
against a rotten sheep crook, tied down
and left to die in Lilliput.

THE WHITE BIRD

The light comes back.
The light always comes back.

No need, I say to myself,
to creep into a nutshell —
that won't keep the light
from coming back.

The white bird
lay dead on my doorstep.
Was it a dove? I don't think so.
It lay there
like the sorrows of the world.

No need, I say to myself,
to make a cave and
hide in it. That won't keep the rain
from coming back, from
ending a dry season.

Scavengers took away
the white dove, if it was one.

No need, I say to myself,
to be glad of its beauty. That won't keep
the sorrows of the world
from coming back
pitiful and beautiful
like a white bird
that might be a dove.

BOOKWORM

I open the second volume
of a rose
and find it says, word for word,
the same as the first one.

The waves of the sea
annoy me, they bore me;
why aren't they divided
in paragraphs?

I look at the night
and make nothing of it —
those black pages
with no print.

But I love the gothic script
of pinetrees and
on the pond the light's
fancy italics.

And the cherry tree's petals —
they make
a sweet lyric, I appreciate
their dying fall.

But it's strange, girl, how I come back
from the library of everything
to stare and stare at
the closed book of you.

When will you open to me
and show me the meaning of all
the hard words
in the lexicon of love?

UGLY CORNER

In my mind you stand guard
outside the bleakest wall,
outside a mean, evil building
that terrifies and attracts me.

You keep me from going in.
But sometimes I hear muffled cries
inside it,
where I am torturing you.

There will be no end to these cries
or to my hearing them
since no torture will ever make you
betray yourself.

AFTER HIS DEATH

It turned out
that the bombs he had thrown
raised buildings:

that the acid he had sprayed
had painfully opened
the eyes of the blind.

Fishermen hauled
prizewinning fish
from the water he had polluted.

We sat with astonishment
enjoying the shade
of the vicious words he had planted.

The government decreed that
on the anniversary of his birth
the people should observe
two minutes pandemonium.

A NOISE OF STUMBLES

Stones in the throat make the hill burn sing.
Without you to choke me, my life would be
A sliding silence. This is the noise I make,
Bickering over your image: for your own sake.

A blundering noise, a noise made out of stumbles
And bawled out broadcast, decorating space
With interruptions. How can it be so gay
That's caused by you and me and gravity?

Sometimes I pull my moorland over me
As hill burns do and gallop in its shade;
Yet still you'll hear me, if you bend your brow,
Go chuckling underground: as I do now.

WORDS IN NOWHERE

With you not here what have I not to say?
I beat my mind dazed on the space between us.
— I'd write you; but the words have gone away.

The words gone? No: they bulge so in my net
I can't haul them up from the great depth between us
No matter how the stretched ropes fray and fret.

And my mind, rejecting limits as it must do,
Mindlessly rages through the time between us
In search of the where and when that make up you.

Yet all this shows, when all's not said or done,
That what's between us is all that's between us —
Our single quarrel that proves that we have none.

A SORT OF EDEN

The poem climbed down from the word-tree,
careful as a parrot,
hoping it was not a parrot.

She, beside the light-tree,
shed her own radiance
inwards.

Under the earth-tree I picked up
the poem. It was a quiet
brown one.

I gave it to her, and it became
the gayest, the gaudiest brown
bird in the garden.

MIDNIGHTS

In any midnight blood bubbles
into ferocious flowers that eat the darkness and crawl
on the sleeper's skin. That safe chair
releases its ghost; it climbs the wall like a louse
and like a daddy long legs hangs from the ceiling
by one toe. Hear how the pillow ferments.
See how the picture on the wall turns into some other
hanged thing, not dead yet. And the window,
that pale psychiatrist, stands watching it all
and coming to dreadful decisions.

And in any midnight blood runs through its narrow streets
shouting the marvellous news: the sleeper's mouth
smiles and his hand half closes to hold
the shape that means perfect. Green wavers of light
spill from the cornices like Spring, like happiness,
like the tenderest of new beginnings. The bed
stands sturdy, its solid block of space
fraternal with everything, holding the sleeper still
in his safest of selves.

And every morning is a landing
at a new airport, is a congregation and scattering of people,
in whose luggage
are undeclared midnights which they will exchange
secretly and without knowing it. A look
is an orchid, a word is a knife, a gesture
a lamentable crying in sunlight. And the midnights wait, each
    one
a fable of the past, each one
a rehearsal of the future.

16

JULY LANDING

The *Eilean Glas,* engine full ahead,
slavers through the sea, wolfishly
making for its lair
at Lochinver. It brushes aside
the sparkling splinters of water.

The day is wildernesses, all
desolate and lovely . . .
As monumental as a monument
a blonde sheltie drowsily stares
through filmstar eyelashes
at the road hemstitched on the skirt
of a mountain. Somewhere
a lamb laments
with the voice of desolation.

On the sand at Achmelvich
six sandpipers play tig
with the Minch, that
keeps casting up and withdrawing
a rinse of soiled lace infested
with sandgrains.

And round Stoer Point swirls
a typhoon of gulls and, under it, the *Eilean Glas*
grinning through the water
till it comes to rest at the pier
in a green seethe of watery
mushrooms and catherine wheels
and the engine stops
with a clap of silence.

GIVE OR TAKE

I approximately approach you and arrive
approximately there. You make
a Pisgah of every place there is.

What do I do with this message? Do I tie it
to a pigeon? Do I translate it into a geometry
of semaphores? Or trust the osmosis of love?

Although you tore up my past and scattered it,
still singing, on that dark stream,
I feel old, you fill me with histories.

Journeys and tribes crowd my narrow place
with sad enrichments. When you look at me
you make me deserve to be me.

Then you enlarge me, you create
a neighbourhood for me to be in
where I stand, peeping from Pisgah.

Comical. But what's comical
in a mobile whose two parts
threaten to, but never kiss?

I would bang approximations together.
What destructions there might be — but what
sparks, what harmonious sonorities!

I AND MY THOUGHTS OF YOU

Remember that old thorn bush
amazed by
its one flower?

If I stood by it, would it be diminished
as an image must be when
it stands beside
what it's an image of?

TWO RINGS

You gave her a ring.
You slid its platinum non-shine
on her finger.

It slowly changed.
It grew, to enclose you both.

She stands inside it
with a little smile on her face,
deftly avoiding
the heavy horns with which
you try to gore
that insulting elegance,
that implacable grace.

SUNSET PLOUGHING

The ploughhorse leaning through the red haze
shuttles also a field without fences,
a gay one, mine. I keep it
inside my skull.

Close up:
his chest gleams, his head
hammers; dragonish steam
jets down from his nostrils.

Long shot:
on the field of my mind
reddening towards another sunset
he shuttles, across and back and across,
adding rib after rib
to that black corduroy.

FALLING ASLEEP BY THE FIRE

Prince Charlie the Bonny Prince
put on his cloak of blood and the room filled
with caves and dark woods.

A voice became Homer — Patroclus
clashed to the ground, and before me flitted
the white wand of soft Circe.

(Outside on the wet road cars made
their glissading sound and a sparrow spoke
in its Toll Cross voice.)

A tall woman of white water glided into the room.
She crossed Loch Scionascaig and vanished
through a painting by Hamish Lawrie.

The island was full of strange noises. — Go away,
Caliban. With a chair for guts, Miranda
smiled at someone off-stage.

(A coal crashed softly. Somewhere
a light bleared through a fog of sleep.
Someone's head rolled sideways.)

And footsteps with no feet went up and down the room.
They fell slower and slower, slower and slower
as the hemlock mounted.

PRISM

The whole forest is illustrations
in a book of botany.
But on the crest of a tree
a myth makes the moonlight glitter
on the carving of chairs, on printing presses,
on the miracle of ink.

The whole city
is a code in a foreign language.
But a fable glows on a street lamp
and someone draws a thread
towards the Minotaur, someone writes
in biblical ledgers
a forty-year wandering. Circe
draws a curtain aside.

A fairytale rustles in a dark room
and a girl weeps for what she has lost
and for what she will never have — she weeps
because rat is rat, Prince Prince,
and toad toad.

DUDE

With goldmines in each corner,
Halcyons making ridiculous all my seas,
    Breakfasts with angels, cruises
    Through laughing Hesperides;

One season, and it all summer,
And doom with a wreath of flowers to dance for me,
    With suns on my rubied fingers,
    Stars gartered below each knee;

I giggle my tall love for you,
I stilt my praises, bow with a wooing grace
    And have no word of mourning
    To shade your turning face,

But, glass of your smiling fashion,
Saunter in bliss and, quizzing the natives there,
    Discover them all your subjects
    With gold straws in their hair.

OLD MAPS AND NEW

There are spaces
where infringements are possible.
There are notices that say:
Trespassers will be welcome.

Pity leaks through the roof
of the Labour Exchange.
In the Leader's pocket,
wrapped in the plans for the great offensive,
are sweets for the children
and a crumpled letter.

There are spaces still to be filled
before the map is completed —
though these days it's only
in the explored territories
that men write, sadly,
Here live monsters.

SPARROW

He's no artist.
His taste in clothes is more
dowdy than gaudy.
And his nest — that blackbird, writing
pretty scrolls on the air with the gold nib of his beak,
would call it a slum.

To stalk solitary on lawns,
to sing solitary in midnight trees,
to glide solitary over gray Atlantics —
not for him: he'd rather
a punch-up in a gutter.

He carries what learning he has
lightly — it is, in fact, based only
on the usefulness whose result
is survival. A proletarian bird.
No scholar.

But when winter soft-shoes in
and these other birds —
ballet dancers, musicians, architects —
die in the snow
and freeze to branches,
watch him happily flying
on the O-levels and A-levels
of the air.

In such falsities, she said,
I recognise your loving truth.
I hated her for it.

When you stay away, she said,
I forgive you, for I know
you're longing to come back.
I hated her for that, too.

When you hurt me, she said,
I know you're hurting not me
but the world.
Pretentious fool.

I can't leave her
for I secretly know
she knows she is lying.
This adds her hurt
to my guilt.

How can so helpless a thing as truth
survive
so many wounds?

FROM WHERE? ✓

Into what shallows of shade
have you gone, teaching them
the mystery of movement? Your face,
between dark callipers of hair,
fades from me, every minute
fades from me into places whose distance
is measured by no miles.

The crinkle of dead leaves
and the singing of a bird in long evenings
are the music I send after you;
A dying fire is your haunting sun.

The world goes on creating
nearnesses and distances
without sighing,
without shrugging its shoulders,
without measuring.

And I walk in it, mourning
the metamorphosis of place,
the death of number,
the illness of time.

In that happy place where you are
your laughter is followed
by my silence.

GULLS ON A HILL LOCH

They resent our arrival, they rise like big snowflakes
blown up in a swirl. They tilt and dive, make sudden
accelerations and effortless towerings, or float, dead still,
offering us
two stony eyes hung between angelic elbows.
They draw diagrams in the air and score them out,
they unravel the sense of pattern.

And all the time the crying, the cackling, the objurgations
in that impossible language! — some
like the cries a shell would make,
or a corkscrew singing in the morning,
or the leading contralto in a choir of tombstones,
or a shell-less egg, or a terrified slate,
or the hinges of a door in the Hospital for the Insane,
or a moonbeam mewing in its forest, or an icicle
arguing with an icicle.
But mostly they are mad, and defiant,
those Gothic scritches and yells and opulent
ululations, compulsively
tearing the air at the seams or yodelling
from a precipice of space.

When we leave, they land on the water,
shrugging and sipping, affronted, glad
to see the back of us, who go downhill
into a summer evening, observing such sanities
as hens — fat dowagers bowing and scraping —
eight swallows clothespegged on a telephone wire
and the village bull, as usual, pretending to be Jove.

ODD MAN OUT

So green's my colour, though my country is
Gray stone, gray water.
(I hate a man who calls a country his.)

I watch red minds absolved from bodies go
In my gray weather,
Will-o'-the-wisping, fading as they glow.

Or bodies hulking hugely through the air
Mindlessly wander,
Shagging with browns and blues the grayness there.

Sometimes the bold sun, happening to pass by,
Blushes, just pinker,
The stone, the water and the drowning sky.

What's that to a man whose helpless knowledge is
Green is his colour?
(I hate a man who calls a colour his.)

So, like a bird that, perking up his song,
Denies it's winter,
I say green, green, green, green: and get along.

MOMENT MUSICAL IN ASSYNT

A mountain is a sort of music: theme
And counter theme displaced in air amongst
Their own variations.
Wagnerian Devil signed the Coigach score;
And God was Mozart when he wrote Cul Mor.

You climb a trio when you climb Cul Beag.
Stac Polly — there's a rondo in seven sharps,
Neat as a trivet.
And Quinag, rallentando in the haze,
Is one long tune extending phrase by phrase.

I listen with my eyes and see through that
Mellifluous din of shapes my masterpiece
Of masterpieces:
One sandstone chord that holds up time in space —
Sforzando Suilven reared on his ground bass.

GAPS

I remember mostly
there are so many things
I do not remember

left behind on a bare mountain
like the blaeberries
I did not pick

as lost to me
as the trout in Loch More
I did not fish for.

And I grieve for the emptiness
they should have filled —
like the one

made by the words
I did not speak
to you.

FRUSTRATED VIRTUOSO

In the corner of Crombie's field
the donkey gets madder every minute. I listen
to his heehawing
seesawing and imagine
the round rich note
he wants to propel into space,
a golden planet of sound orbiting
to the wonder of the world.

No wonder
when he hears what comes out of
that whoopingcough trombone
his eyes fill with tears
and his box head drops
to lip the leaves of thistles — accepting that
they're all he deserves.

BEHIND A SHUT DOOR

I see a stone.
It makes a building, I see it rise
From a cloud of earth to its own invented skies.

I know a man —
A winding column of refugees
From the past, bowed under his chattel of centuries.

I hear a bird,
And testaments in a cage of song
Cry cruel love; they sigh and cry How long?

I watch a child
Whose weeping is all there is. I say Yes,
Yes, yes to that terrible loneliness.

I take no heed —
A crime that every day I commit
And hate and hate myself because of it.

INWARD BOUND

On the Calton Hill
the twelve pillars
of this failed Parthenon
    made more Greek by the cargo boat
    sailing between them
    on the cobwebby water of the Firth
should marry nicely with the Observatory
in the way complements do
    each observing the heavens
    in its different way.
Yet these pillars fit better
with the man sat scrunched between them —
even his raincoat might have warded off the weather
all the way from Thebes. The scrip by his side
is filled with Scotch olives.

The illumination of new problems
burns on the tiderace that headlongs
straight as Princes Street
from dawn to dusk — as the sideslipping sun
makes flares of the windows of the North British Hotel
    they'll die back through blankness into windows
    and prove, tomorrow, illuminations
    are not answers.

And the man between the pillars
will be replaced by another
making through the windings of the world
towards his Ithaca and proving
there's no end to the windings
or the journeyings.

The Castle pretends No,
as though, having choked the flume of a volcano,
it could make history gag
by sticking in its throat
        forgetting that once
        round its harsh crag wheeled
        spent crossbow arrows
        that splashed in the Nor' Loch whose water
        translated them to ducks.

Swans still go over, seaplaning down
to Dunsappie, and geese
squeezing the bulbs of oldfashioned motor horns
waver high over the Queen's Bath House
their flat bills
pointing straight to Benbecula
        a knotless thread of journeying
        one of a web too tangled
        to have a centre.

Journeys. Mine were
as wide as the world is
from Puddocky to Stockbridge
        minnows splinter in a jar
        and a ten-inch yacht
        in the roaring forties of Inverleith Pond
        crumples like a handkerchief
till the web enlarged
        choked once with a zeppelin
        that dropped the beginning of the end of the world
        on the Grassmarket
to enclose places that grew two selves
        their own and the one I made of it
and people that became two multitudes
        their own and the one I invented

36

and ideas
        whose war of attrition still goes on
        in my only skull — how many casualties
        are marked with no cross
        in the dark backward.

Dark as the stairs and closes of the Canongate
and the West Bow. They smell of piss
that used to smell of piss and pomanders
and are gothic and gloomy enough
for a weak mind
to hallucinate the shadows
with shades —
with the perukes and cloaks
of foppish and lousy gangsters —
the costume jewellery
in poor bedraggled Scotland's diadem.

No journey is ever ended
        Greyfriars and the melancholy double-blanks
        in Warriston Kirk Yard
        are no answers to that
or reversible.
And most haunting of all
are the ones that were never made.
        Out of my speech
        I trespassed over the border
        into Gaelic and glimpsed
        facts and the decoration of facts
        that now only glimmer in my mind
        like a coin at the bottom of a well.

Such a long way back
such a long way in
        when the famous killers were in Chicago

and Glasgow was a mean city
and Welsh miners sang in London streets
and Scotch potatoes were lifted by Irish girls
when the world to me
was Heaven in its infancy all rosy and
spangled with islands. I
fishing for cuddies off Craig Lexie
going for a few sheep
to an island off an island off an island
was a millionaire of sunlight and summer winds
freeman of kingdoms behind a kingdom
far traveller among spinningwheels
explorer of songs
and without knowing it a miser
stuffing the bag of my mind
with sovereigns
I've been spending ever since.

What water ever flashed
        ever flashes
like the water in the Red Well
and what mysteries of distance
and unguessable arrivals
were not crammed in the hold of the *Eilean Glas*
anchored in Scalpay bay
and streamed by the tide in a due line
pointing to the Clisham.

(The fishergirls sang on the pier.
Their songs had nothing to do
with the blood and the guts of herring.

Though one had no thought for me
to this day when I think of her
I feel new wounds

remembering
that flashing knife,
those bandaged fingers.)

Such a journey back
such a journey in —
it expands it brings closer
places and non-places
          as though to journey
          in a stone —
          through dreams and their extensions —
          across the border of the farthest idea.
These things come down into
the region of the possible — I feel
I could fly without feathers
          — and no talk of Icarus.

Every step
is a moonlanding, my feet sink
in unpredictables and astonishments.
They carry me to where
I look down on the brawny continents
and the slipshod oceans fixed by distance
into stillness.

Darkness I love darkness I am motored
by darkness
          the soil flows smoothly over
          my two-way fur, I paddle it
          aside
which has its dusky galaxies
the glimmerings of darkness in darkness
on which someone
will make a glimmer-landing
and send messages up

as new flowers.
     A shape disturbs some fibres
     inside my head with bracts
     and foetal stamens and tinted vapour
     of possible flowers smelling
     of a time to come, of a distance
     not yet thought of.

Yet that leaf
     on the branch —
         in the pool —
             in my mind —
signed itself in triplicate
and of the three statements it made
I could read only the third
and it the most corrupt.

I can't make myths I can't make fables.
When I try to invent one
a true crow swallows real cheese
and a real fox
doesn't like grapes anyway.
Yet I am peeked at by possibilities that vanish
when I turn to stare at them, as though a fable
were signalling desperately from the future to
now.
     Possibilities! said the man to me
     by the Blackford Pond. — They put in one hand
     the rose of all the world and
     in the other a tick wrapped in a parcel.
     I agreed, gravely, and watched, gravely, a swan
     floating like a lotus
     with a white snake in it.

And no talk of Icarus.

— Yet for one Icarus
there was a Daedalus.
And for each who remembers
the pitching, the alighting of that maniac man-bird
how many remember
the curled cloud
the ship sailing by
and the white, sudden
tombstone of water.

Now by the Nelson Monument
I die another of the innumerable deaths
life can be made to seem to consist of
        the easiest ones, the ones with resurrections
and cheerfully thankfully bequeath to myself
journeys remembered
to be divided amicably between
my romantic my classical
my Gothic my Georgian
my orchestral my plainsong
me.

THE LITTLE FALLS POOL

Giggle and thump —
the water does both at once.
The stone it creases over
smiles like a mandarin,
porcelained with water.
Upstream, a posse
of baby mergansers
squatters, eleven squeaks in line,
across a sliding prairie of water.
It all makes happiness
seem easy.

There's a cloud
in the space between us.
Cruelty roams there,
cruelty and desolation.
There are sad minds
in the space between us
(and happiness, and happiness).
But where you are
and where I am
there is room only
for happiness natural as this water
creased over a stone. I watch
the eight fluff-balls running on its surface
with love, knowing they'll reach
the dark overhang
where their mother waits for them.

COLD SONG

The doctor gazed
at the sack of guts passing
and saw
my pretty girl.

The lawyer looked at
a ringless finger
and saw my
pretty girl.

The professor noticed
eyes quick with intelligence
and
saw my pretty girl.

I met my pretty girl
and saw an intelligent
sack of guts with
a ringless finger.

AT LAST

Sure I can walk
under your sombrero of clouds.
Sure I can sail
over your hissing keel
that makes bubbles where no bubbles should be.
What's to keep me
from prancing elegantly
in your red-heeled shoes?

I choose not to do it,
having clouds of my own
and a boat with cracked rowlocks
and feet that are moccasined in blood
with walking to you,
with walking away from you.

OLD MAN

He eats his past. The few days left to him
have no nourishment in them
till they've happened.
— How greedily he eats it —

stone bird on the castle gate
that began as a phoenix
and has been weathered
into a vulture.

MOON-LANDING

The rind of Newton's apple
was hard as a mason's hand;
yet the apple exploded, its pulp
spattered minds in closets
then minds outside closets.
That was the beginning.

Now two minds, hard
as silicon, glittering as quartz,
fall logically on moondust;
and blind stars and dwarf stars
are trees of apples and the forests
of galaxies make audible
their shaking leaves.
In a mind's midnight
they rustle and shine
as threatening as logic,
as beautiful as revelation.

MARRIAGE BED

The mountainy air going dry across the sea
Will come back in the morning
So soft and damp my hair will find new curls:
They won't cheat me to thinking I'm reborn.

Big moths, washed-blue, flutter their Kleenex wings
A foot above the grasses.
Their blunt gun-turret heads are masks of gold.
They shake like water bounced in a narrow glass.

A hundred yards away a corncrake keeps
Pressing the starter button —
The song won't fire. I wince to think what skulks
In my homely hayfield mind. (That's still uncut.)

In the white fluttering appears a golden one.
She scarabs on a nettle.
White wings land on her and crawl underneath —
And there are years and years to squander yet.

RETURN

Rings glowed. Gem stones underground
hid in their dark cloaks. The sky was mineral
with squeaks of light, with nail-scratchings.
And the bosomy river glided by
full of rings and gem stones and trailed stars.

It was a night for tall-hatted wizards
and children with blank eyes
and cats spitting in the black forge of a tree.
It was a night for fat marrows
to forage grunting through the blackberry thickets,
for the moon to be singing
Ophelia songs . . . A mist steamed up
like the ghosts of millions of pearls.

But a hand of water
clasped mine, a rough bark
caught at my sleeve.
I was waylaid by a stone and stumbled
into where geometries
mutely displayed their curves and angles
and distances kept their places
and the path by the river led
through glitters and glooms to
clear definitions,
to dictionaries of miracles.

NEW TABLES

A mathematician who came to his senses
thought deeply
(putting his finger to his forehead,
putting his finger through his forehead)
and wrote:

One robust curse equals
two shrieks, four groans:
One hour with you
equals every convalescence:
One boy on a scooter equals
transport:
One Yes equals ten
commandments:
One new life equals
a million old deaths:
Love equals
equal.

The world read this, stupefied
with admiration
and went on dying and laughing
and shedding
logarithms of tears.

A TRUTH IN TWO HALVES

A bulge of light sits on that shelf
As though the idea of a jar
Had thickened and become a self.

Half self, half light. I stare and can't
Be easy with what seems at once
Visitor and visitant.

I know the light won't take it back,
Dissolving it before my eyes.
— Yet turn the light out. In the black

Cube of a room, I hold the jar
Like a fish under water and
My world is not where my hands are.

OLD POET ON A BEACH

The sea had worn the stone into
a brown jug, stubby and beautiful
with a salty sparkle in the brown.

He had been worn, too,
by rubbing time, by shingles of people.
The bones of his mind had a new shape.

Yet what had been discarded
by these indefatigable sculptors
was invisibly at work.

It had become them,
transforming stones,
grinding new shapes of people.

COUNTRY DANCE

The room whirled and coloured
and figured itself with dancers.
Another gaiety seemed born of theirs
and flew like streamers
between their heads and the ceiling.

I gazed, coloured and figured,
down the tunnel of streamers —
and there, in the band, an old fiddler
sawing away in the privacy
of music. He bowed lefthanded and his right hand
was the wrong way round. Impossible.
But the jig bounced, the gracenotes
sparkled on the surface of the tune.
The odd man out, when it came to music,
was the odd man in.

There's a lesson here, I thought, climbing
into the pulpit I keep in my mind.
But before I'd said Firstly brethren, the tune
ended, the dancers parted, the old fiddler
took a cigarette from the pianist, stripped off
the paper and ate the tobacco.

TREE HUNG WITH FAIRY LIGHTS

It's not additions but extensions give
A thing its further self,
Changed from within:
Blossom's a sort of leaf, as nail is skin.

But decoration contradicts the tree.
I love you best (and know
It's love, not lust)
When clothed in nothing but your altered dust.

SOMEWHERE, SOMETIME

A little snow begins to fall.
My hat catches on the Plough.
I am nowhere where I can be seen.

My hand is hot with stroking Virgo.
The people I walk through
remain undisturbed, the streets
they walk through disturb me.
A little snow continues to fall.

Scorpio hisses at me, I crawl
into Orion's scabbard.
A face in the traffic lifts up
and barks at the snow that
goes on falling.

I'm going out of my mind, but into
what? Why should that café
not say Hello, that policeman
not reprove me? What right have I
not to exist? Where is the way out
from this snow that keeps on falling
from the Dog, the Crab, the plunging Scales?

MESSAGE

As though my opaque life were in a tumbler
I stared at it, I gave it a swirl,
and could see nothing but opacity.

Even the sea beside me might have been
iron rolling in. Every molecule
marched at attention.

I thought of the distance between us
filled with predestined acres and the stiff bars
of miles.

Then the sunset turned a tree
into a macaw and lovingly drew the outline of a sheep
with astonishing silver.

And I thought of how many ways there are
of thinking of you, and gave up
except for that one.

And the tumbler
had a gleam in it. It rocked
with the beginnings of illuminations.

They showed me
dissolving acres, soft miles, and the military sea
clowning ashore.

The light in that glass
was one with the first one that was
divided from the darkness.

DREAM SCHOLAR

What is a dream worth?
One drop of new blood?
Two wings?
The sea cooped in a seashell?
A rose of corruption?
    — You dream of entanglements of thickets
    where nightingales straight from stock
    objurgate, wheedle, firecracker, burr,
    and glades are drifted through
    by figures of unconscionable hauteur
    and speechless beauty. I dream
    of a tooth torn out, of ripped gums.
    Whose castration complex
    is more complex?

When the ministry of brain transport
resigns and
the flyovers, cloverleafs, stop-and-goes in the skull
vanish with it, what
short-cuts, what head-on collisions,
what screechings of sad ambulances,
what folk fun at the roundabouts.
    — You lift a cat and snuff the cupped petals
    of his face. The stone on your finger
    chimes. The weasel at your breast
    eats his way in, feet scuffling. And I
    watch a salmon rise — not salmon, but
    an anatomised man, knees horribly
    bent — or step from a window
    and fall up and up forever.
    Are the disarticulations of your mind
    more articulate than mine?

What is a dream worth?
A day in the life of Walter Mitty?
A return ticket to Gagaland?
A princely toad?
A Tom who's praised for his peeping?
      — You talk of seedy rooms
      where on immaculate and glowing thrones
      your smirking selves
      nod amnesties, smile pardons —
      in a royal collusion they call back
      absconding cornfields and fill slum kitchens
      with bread that tastes of hymns.
      I talk
      of sea-shingle applause, of Goliath
      concertina'd to the ground, of the lusty woman
      tasting of dew.
      Is your inferiority complex
      superior to mine?

The books are wrong about Grace.
It does not descend. It does not alight.
It emerges from cracks and filthy cellars
and old coats on the backs of chairs.
A crooked self hauls it into existence
from the hot belly of envy.
It hallucinates water
into lying wine and the drinker,
with a holy, simpering smile,
pats cancer on the head,
gives prizes to bereavement
and plots his straight course to heaven
through prisons and battlefields.
      — You dream of holy receptions
      in a gold and glittering air
      where trees bow to you, rocks fawn

round your wicked knees and a weight of doom
suddenly balloons up, leaving you
light as innocence. I sit,
(Genghis Khan of street corners)
my pickthank fingers turned to harps, my ribs
strumming with trivial crimes,
by the euphoric glassy sea.

I can meet you
in my dream,
but I in my dream
can never meet you in yours.

So what are dreams worth,
that drift across the sleepless
vision of reality? I ask it and ask it,
staring
into your dreaming eyes.

FAMILY

The father raised words
like gentle whiplashes. His eyes
were Mosaic with a dubious wisdom. Boyhood
was a crime he had once committed.

The mother wept secretly inside
her joy. She knew every new word
was an argument against her, that the first steps
were the beginning of a long journey.

The little boy's eyes were frightened
but would not close. He stared
beyond the serpent in the apple tree
to the round sweet dangerous apple.

SPELLED

You conjure white rabbits —
but from a witch's hat.
You lead me in beautiful circles
widdershins.

How was I to know
the words you speak to me come
from the devil's dictionary?

When I warp them straight
it's you who will cry — but worse,
it's I will be sorry.

DOWN AND DOWN

Therefore I fall
in a way that never misses the target
like all the marvellous fallers
Icarus Phaethon (Lucifer).

The depth I fall into
is cruelly just light enough
for me to see it;
else how know I was falling?

I had only the usual
pride, the usual ambition.
Icarus Phaethon Lucifer
I will be no legend.

When I reach the bottom
of bottomlessness, there will be
no broken wings beside me,
no chariot of the sun.

And no crystal battlements
will infinitely shine above me.
I will be left with only
the loneliness of falling.

IN A MIST

The mountains fold and move.
I'm not quite lost. The thing that troubles me
Is that the easiest way out
Is not the one that's easiest to see.

I know just where you are.
But how to get there when lochs change their place
And the familiar track
Squirms like an adder into the heather bushes?

I curse my senses: and speak
Into the mist: Stay where you are, please stay —
I've got my compass yet.
It'll get me to you, if not by the easiest way.